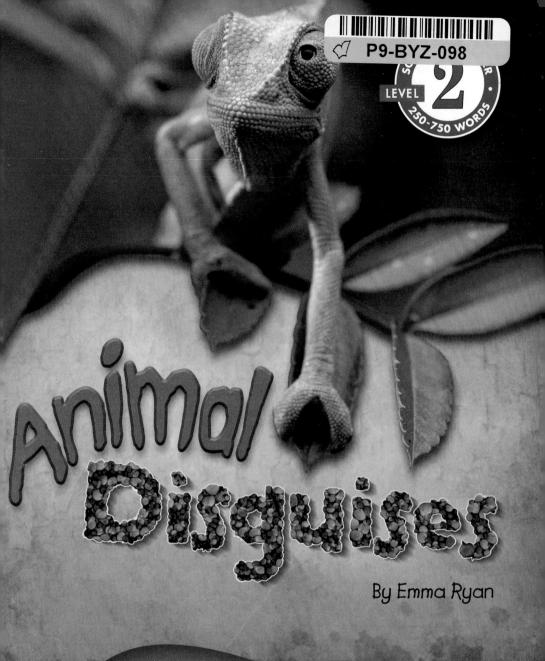

Animal Disguises

By Emma Ryan

SCHOLASTIC INC.

New York   Toronto   London   Sydney

Auckland   Mexico City   New Delhi   Hong Kong

Photo Credits
Front cover [top]: © Stephen Dalton/Nature Picture Library; [bottom]
© Brainstorm 1962/iStockphoto; Back cover: © Missing35mm/iStockphoto;
title page: © Stephen Dalton/Nature Picture Library; p. 3: © OfiPlus/
Shutterstock; pp. 4-5: © VisualCommunications/iStockphoto; p. 6:
© Missing35mm/iStockphoto; p. 7: © Peter Leahy/Shutterstock; p. 9:
© Orionmystery@flickr/Shutterstock; p. 10: © Pawel Kielpinski/Shutterstock;
pp. 12-13: © Iggy1108/iStockphoto; p. 15: © Pokergecko/iStockphoto;
p. 16: © Brainstorm 1962/iStockphoto; p. 17: © Visuals Unlimited/
Getty Images; pp. 18-19: © Oxford Scientific/Getty Images; pp. 20-21:
© Science Faction/Getty Images; pp. 22-23: © Georgette Douwma/Getty
Images; p. 24: © Frederic Pacorel/Getty Images; p. 25: © Dan Schmitt/
iStockphoto; p. 26: © Science Faction Jewls/Getty Images; pp. 28-29:
© Shoemcfly/iStockphoto; p. 31: © Wolfgang Steiner/iStockphoto.

ISBN 978-0-545-31763-4

10 9 8 7 6 5 4 3 2 1   11 12 13 14 15/0

Printed in the U.S.A   40
First printing, September 2011

Did you know some animals play hide-and-seek? Chameleons, like this one, use camouflage to blend into their surroundings and disguise themselves. Camouflage helps keep animals safe from predators. What other animals use camouflage?

Arctic hares have a thick layer of fur to keep them warm in cold temperatures. Their fur changes color from brown during the summer to bright white during the winter.

Can you spot the hare?

Check page 32 to see if you're right!

The change helps them hide from predators like wolves and foxes in the ice and snow.

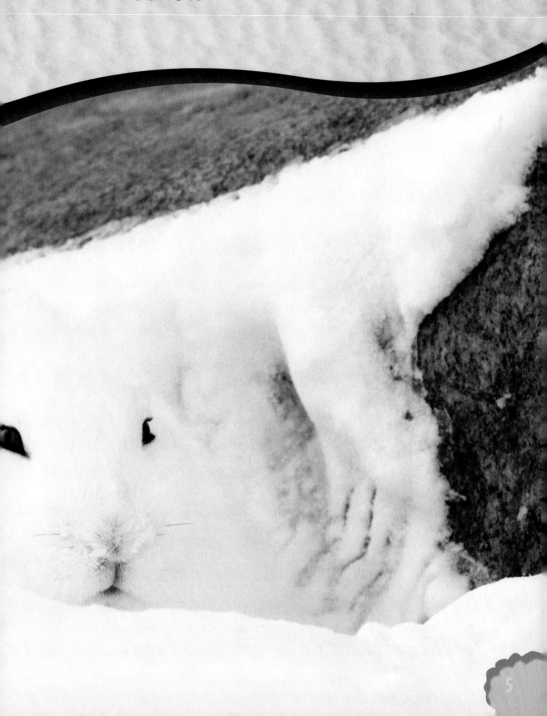

Barn owls can be found almost anywhere in the world. They have white, heart-shaped faces, spotted chests, and light brown feathers on their backs and wings. These feathers are perfect camouflage against the barns and tree trunks where they usually live.

Instead of blending in, owl butterflies' disguises make them easier to see. Owl butterflies have an animal-looking eyespot on each wing. Looking like a larger animal helps keep them safe by frightening away predators. They are mostly found in the Amazon rainforest.

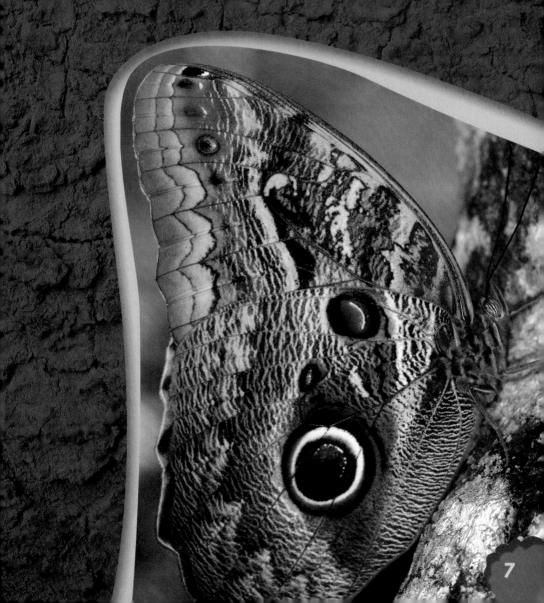

Did you see that leaf move? Look closely . . . it's actually a leaf insect. These tiny creatures live mainly in the jungles of Southeast Asia. They are well-hidden standing still or moving, since their walk looks like a leaf blowing in the wind.

The Malaysian orchid mantis might be beautiful, but can also be deadly! Looking like a flower helps the mantis catch and eat other insects by tricking them into coming closer. Its legs look like petals, and it will flatten its body out when threatened to look even more like an orchid.

Can you spot the insect?

Check page 32 to see
if you're right!

The stick insect is almost impossible to
see among the twigs where it lives.

They can be found in tropical areas and are usually green or brown in color.

Who spies on flies? Frogs!
Frogs also use camouflage to hide
from danger. Gray tree frogs look a lot
like the tree trunks they hang out on.

Green frogs can easily hide among tree leaves and swamps without being seen.

Pygmy seahorses are tiny creatures that rarely grow more than one inch long! They can be different colors and found in the Pacific Ocean. Their camouflage works so well, they were only discovered after the coral they lived on was taken to an aquarium.

Can you spot
the seahorses?

Check page 32 to see
if you're right!

Leafy sea dragons live in the oceans off of Australia and are experts at hide-and-seek. They are usually yellow, green, or brown in color and are able to float among seaweed and kelp undetected.

The mimic octopus could be called a secret agent of the sea. It has the ability to look like eels, sea snakes, rays, and jellyfish!

Scientists think this sea creature changes its appearance depending on what type of predator it's trying to hide from.

Sting rays are usually found in shallow water. They like to hang out on the seafloor partially buried in the sand.

Their coloring and flat bodies help them hide from predators and find food like shrimp, fish, and worms without being seen.

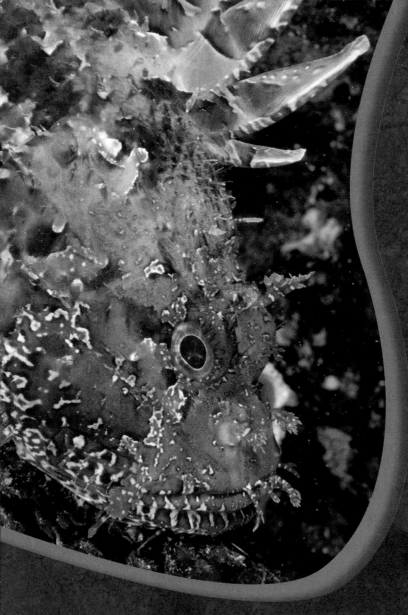

Watch out for the scorpion fish! They are carnivores that eat other fish to survive, and their fins are poisonous. Some species are sandy in color, but others are colorful and blend into the surrounding coral.

Cuttlefish have small structures filled with colored ink that form different patterns and textures that make them look like coral or algae. The ink helps them hide from predators and can be used to attack creatures that get too close.

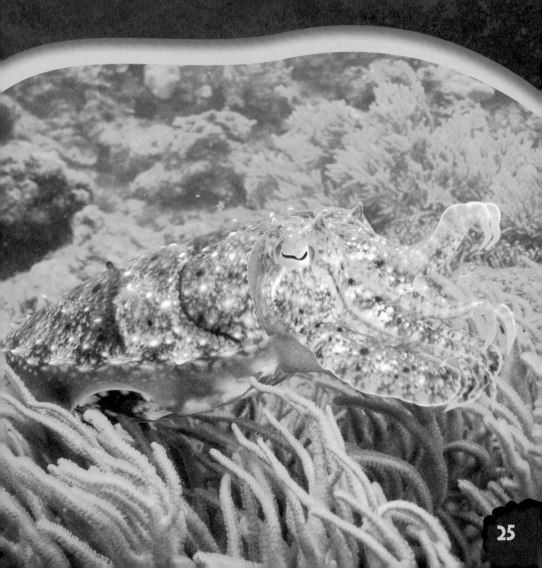

Can you spot the crab?

Check page 32 to see
if you're right!

The decorator crab is a master of disguise! This tricky crustacean attaches other sea creatures like algae, anemones, and sponges to its body as camouflage.

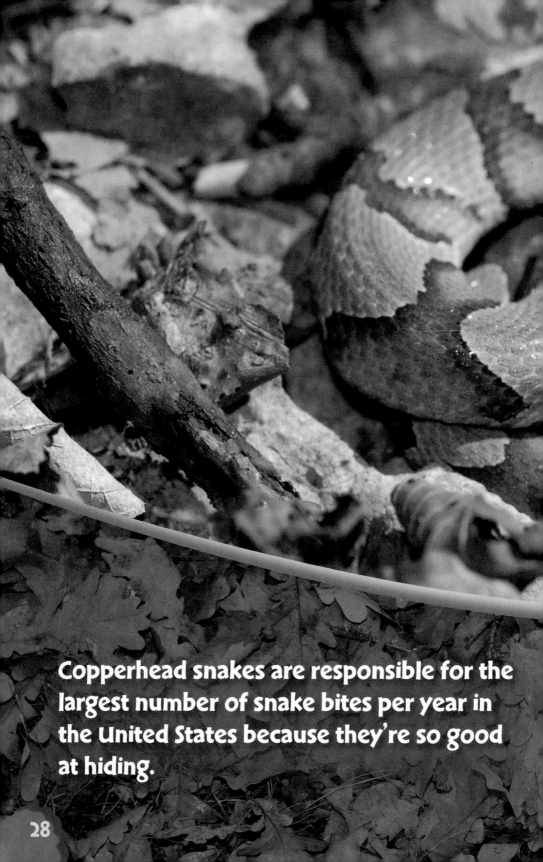

Copperhead snakes are responsible for the largest number of snake bites per year in the United States because they're so good at hiding.

These poisonous snakes have patterned scales in shades of brown. They can be found almost anywhere and like to hide among rocks, dried leaves, wood piles, and in gardens.

You might not think the king of the jungle needs to hide from anyone, but lions use camouflage to help them hunt and catch their prey. Their light brown fur easily blends into the stalks of grass while they hunt for food.

Glossary

Aquarium: A glass tank where fish are held, or a place where visitors can see different types of underwater creatures.

Camouflage: A disguise used for blending in or hiding.

Carnivore: An animal that eats meat.

Coral: An underwater creature that has a stony skeleton and lives in colonies.

Crustacean: A sea creature that has an outer skeleton.

Predator: An animal that hunts other animals for food.

Prey: An animal that is hunted by others animals for food.

Species: One of the groups into which plants and animals are divided.

Did you find all the animals?